Other Books by George Kagawa

A Month of Sundays

Never Say Never

Now You Tell Me

The Last Thing on My Mind

Save The Best For Last

Minding My Own Business

The Irony of it All

Retake

In My View

Getting it Right

Sex and Sensibility for Seniors

2019 © Copyright George Kagawa
Published by Glorybound Publishing, Camp Verde, AZ
SAN 256-4564
10 9 8 7 6 5 4 3 2 1
Printed in the United States of America
KDP ISBN 9781705562963
Copyright data is available on file.
Kagawa, George, 1934-
         Sex and Sensibility for Seniors
1. Self Improvement   2. Senior   I. Title

www.gloryboundpublishing.com

Sex and Sensibility for Seniors

George Kagawa

Glorybound Publishing
Camp Verde, Arizona USA
in the year 2019

To those who
suggested this while slightly drunk,
assuming I knew something about it since
I got married at 77 for the fourth time,
and to my wife Chris, for her optimistic ideas
on spending the wildly imagined royalties,
unaware that self-published books
average under 200 per year per title,
and cost more to publish
than the royalties made on sales.

THANKS TO INDIVIDUALS

Thank you to my friend Annie for suggesting this book even though I feel that I am hardly qualified to talk about this subject.

Thanks also to my wife, Chris for encouraging me and inspiring me every since we have been married.

I also wish to thank Brad and Jen, my children, for supporting my writing all these years.

LETTER FROM THE AUTHOR

I'm 77 and recently married, less than a month ago. For the fourth time. I've had reasonably good health, but like some people my age, have erectile dysfunction. It doesn't dampen my libido, but it does require that I improvise. My bride Chris, a youthful, lusty 75, has a healthy sexual appetite, and I would be remiss if I did not fulfill my conjugal duties. I moved recently from Hawaii to Sedona, Arizona, and have met most of Chris' friends. Some are a few years younger, but most are in their 70s, some in their 60s, a few in their 80s and 90s.

Some have been married for a long, long time, others have been married about ten years. Some are singles and one is in her early 90s, and still active sexually.

We conjecture about their sex lives, and we surmise that some are still hanging in there, some have smoldering ashes but are about ready to have the fire go out, and some are stone cold and haven't been sleeping together for years and years.

I don't insist that sex is important to the senior citizen, whether you're married or not. There are no hard and fast rules; we know couples who have been married for over 40 years and look like they haven't had sex with each other for at least 20 years, and they are making their marriage work. They had problems, but they didn't involve sex – mainly drinking, bad temperaments – but they worked things through and are happy and functionally successful as a married couple.

But since sex is nonetheless an engaging topic and seems to preoccupy our attention quite often, it seems like a good topic for a book, or for social conversation. And since I don't know if we'll be having a friendly shindig soon to talk about it, I may as well write about it.

TABLE OF CONTENTS

Chapter 1

Sex For The Septuagenarian

If we're not doing it, we're either thinking about it (in past, present or future tense) or talking about it, sometimes seriously, sometimes with humor, sometimes as a current event in the papers.

So, most of us are either pre-occupied or occupied with sex. I think it's safe to surmise that seniors are no exception, even if it's referred to as a fond memory from the past, something that they used to engage in but stopped for some reason – they ran out of gas or interest, they turned to hobbies or TV or books, or felt that they were too old to show an active interest in it.

Being a newlywed, I forgot about the clock and the calendar and how I was supposed to feel about sex. I know how I feel about my bride and can't get enough of her, and don't let social convention, "common practice," or ED stifle me. For those much younger who don't read ads for Viagra, Cialis or

Levitra, ED doesn't stand for Doctor of Education. It stands for Erectile Dysfunction. Some people go soft in the head and are stricken with Alzheimer's; many more get soft in the other head and can't get an erection, at least one hard enough and long enough (in terms of time, not inches) to penetrate for intercourse.

Now, you can leave the cap off the toothpaste tube, leave the toilet seat up, and even drink until the wee hours of the morning, and might still keep your marriage going. But if sex is important to your mate and you are charged for assault with a dead weapon, you may not even have a mother-in-law to complain about for long.

This doesn't mean that sex is inherently important to keep a marriage viable, or even a romantic relationship. Chances are, it is, but it doesn't have to be. Whatever a couple is happy with, whatever their core values are in that department, they can make their relationship work regardless of what the armchair psychologists, marriage and family counselors, friends, neighbors and family say. They can and should make their own rules, especially if they're seniors.

For one, they're old enough to know what's best for them. For another, who cares what their adult kids think? Their grand kids and great grand kids probably are more lenient and accepting of whatever their grandma or great-grandma, or grandpa or great-grandpa are doing. At worst, they may be considered crazy but cool, but still loved, not judged or criticized for what may seem like questionable choices or decisions.

Chapter 2

Tantric Sex

Ten days after our wedding, a friend whom I'll call Sally took Chris and me to dinner to the fabulous Enchantment Restaurant in beautiful Boynton Canyon as a wedding gift.

For some inexplicable reason, she thought that we should write a manual about tantric sex for seniors, as if we had specialized talents for that subject matter.

I responded by saying that the only thing close to that which I could write about with any degree of authority was sex tantrums, about pouting and stomping my feet if I didn't have my way, if I wanted something done faster or slower, higher or lower, softer or harder and shrieking in a high-pitched voice, like someone in the terrible two's.

I kidded about some considerations unique to senior citizens, like how they might have to improvise or make modifications if one or both partners used a walker, cane, oxygen tank, wheel chair, or was in a hospital bed.

I suggested the safety considerations applicable to cane users, that using a cane as a surrogate for penile entry could be hazardous since the rubber tip picks up a lot of bacteria, and if a female wanted to use it as a dildo, it would require enormous dexterity and agility or very long limbs to insert it into either orifice. And if they wanted to launch it as a projectile, it would require dexterity, accuracy and precision to hit the intended target with the desired speed, angle of direction, and accuracy.

I suggested that one's own hand, with or without a latex glove, would be simpler and easier to use for self-stimulation and self-enjoyment. There are other avenues to explore, of course. Prolonged, extensive kissing to various parts of the body, moving around in random fashion, not so much in linear fashion from contiguous part to contiguous part. If the body were an atlas, it could be done by skipping "countries" or continents, to introduce the element of delightful surprise.

And the whole area of oral sex opens up exciting new opportunities for adventure and discovery.

More accurately, one could say it opens up hole new opportunities. Words are important to fuel the flow of love and romance, giving new meaning to oral sex. Being able to speak in several languages adds a touch of the exotic, even if it's limited to a few phrases of intimacy and endearment. Being facile with words is helpful even if one only speaks one language, but being able to speak in several tongues is a definite advantage. It also helps to be clever and funny; there are untold advantages in being a cunning linguist.

But enough on this play on words. Sex is not the be-all that ends all, and clearly it is not an absolute requirement for congenial companionship, but it can spice up a couple's life if they are so inclined. And if one happens to be without a partner for an extended period of time, one can learn to temporize or ward off the tensions that come from involuntary abstinence with the use of paraphernalia or self-stimulation. Beware of the woman with an inordinate love of walnuts and who has a large jar full of sticky-feeling quarters; she may have those around to practice privately on her kegels, and is keeping in shape.

Chapter 3

Safe Sex

This is not about contraceptives and birth control, which are usually unnecessary for seniors. STDs and AIDS are usually not a concern (unless you're a senior in Florida, where seniors lead the state in STD frequency).

Safe sex has a different connotation. While this may seem to be a no-brainer, it does require mentioning because injuries to a senior usually take longer to heal and have potentially more serious consequences. In addition, it might be embarrassing explaining to family and friends how the accident occurred.

You may find different venues exciting, offering a change in pace and a cure for boredom. Sex in the outdoors sounds spontaneous and dashing, but there's the risk of being discovered by someone. If it's a stranger who doesn't know you or doesn't recognize you, you can simply cover yourself and get away as quickly as possible. Rather than cover your genitals or your breasts, as you may want to, automatically a better way is to cover your face.

It's not likely that they'll see you in a rest room, look at your genitals, and say, "Hey, didn't I see you at (name of place)?"

Which they might say, if they had seen your face. And even if no one sees you, the fire ants might, and while that might give you a funny story to tell later on, you might not think it's so funny while it's happening.

The living room floor, if carpeted, might still harbor tics and fleas if you have a cat or dog. If bare, the hardwood floor or tile may be too hard to your liking. If so, you can have your partner take to the floor, which you can talk them into by suggesting, "I've always wanted to try it on top." Note: This might apply whether you're a man or a woman.

The dining room table or kitchen counter might sound glamorous and amorous, but even if you have a careful wipe down afterward, if you missed a sticky spot, you can count on your guests or a dog or cat, yours or your guests', finding it and licking it with obvious delight. On both the living room and the dining room table or kitchen counter, any moves that are overly enthusiastic could result in either a fall or a thrust that might be too hard for the tender parts of your body, which might prefer a softer shock absorber.

Other places to avoid are sofas, especially love seats, which might literally cramp your style. The conventional bed, while pedestrian and mundane, is the safest, like a king or queen sized bed. You can get by with a double, but take extra precautions with a twin.

A twin-sized bed, that is, not a fraternal or identical twin, no matter how much you love your family. If you have a headboard, give yourself enough room to avoid banging your head or your partner's against the headboard. For one, it hurts. Secondly, it makes a lot of tell-tale noise.

Stay in the middle of the bed, not too close to the edge, and not too far down where you might topple off the back edge. When your arms and legs are entangled, and you are both nude, a fall could result in some strange injuries that may not only be painful and take along time to recover from and put you out of commission for a while, but would be very difficult to explain, no matter how imaginative you are. No one is likely to believe that you were practicing and learning a new dance, and it was so hot you were practicing in the nude.

Better to be safe than sorry, and unable to have sex until the doctor says you can resume.

Chapter 4

Talking A Good Game

This is mainly targeted for the men, but certainly applicable for women. Foreplay should start from the time you open your eyes in the morning up to and including when you start to engage in sex. The downside is that your whole way of thinking might drastically change, to a point that it will appear, and perhaps rightfully so, that all you can think about is sex.

This might be flattering to your female partner (I imagine it applies to lesbians as well), but your comments and verbal ways of framing your comments and questions might strongly indicate that you have become raunchy and crass, and may even influence your behavior – the way you touch your mate, and where, whether you're in public or not, where, if seen, it would clearly be taken as inappropriate, lewd, or certainly, in poor taste and suggestive of a bad upbringing.

The upside is that your mate will love it, and may even be encouraged to be very open and uninhibited, and forgetting and forgoing her genteel and proper upbringing. As a man, I find it thrilling and flattering to have my mate pat or stroke me when we are out in public, on parts of my body that would excite me when we are alone, let alone in public.

The double entendres, innuendoes, risqué jokes, bad puns, and visual double takes over the most innocuous of remarks will help to keep sex in the forefront and in the consciousness of you two to a point when you retire for the night, or go to bed to "take a nap," you can't help but feel aroused and eager for sex, because you've been talking about it all day.

At that point, it doesn't matter that you're not the greatest lover or the best endowed, she'll treat you as if you were. And if she does, why break the illusion?

Play along with that role, and in the ensuing excitement, you'll believe it too.

Chapter 5

Can You Get Too Much of a Good Thing?

Ronnie, my best golfing buddy when I lived in Hawaii, once told me that he and his late second wife, Clara, were watching an Oprah show in August of 2009, and Dr. Oz was on her show.

The topic was sex, and Oprah asked him, "How often should a couple have sex?"

Dr. Oz said, "About two to four times a week."

Oprah pressed forward and she asked him, "So, in the course of a year, how many times, roughly, would that work out to?"

Dr. Oz paused for a second and said, "About 200 times."

At which point, Clara turned to Ron and said, "Oh oh, looks like you've used up your quota for the year."

Certainly, I don't think there's an optimum

number of times a couple should have sex. It depends on the couple. I don't think I personally will ever feign a headache and say not tonight, dear, I have a splitting headache, but there are times when I am physically breathless and gasping for air, and if my mate ever asked for or suggested more sex, I have had to tell her the truth that I need to catch my breath first, and that I needed a short break.

Sex can be a good cardiac workout, but if you were lifting weights in a gym and wanted to bench press another set with more weights or more reps simply because you had such a great time with the last set, you might be happy and dead with a bar and some weights draped across your chiseled chest.

Life IS short. May as well lengthen it when you can, by being discreet and prudent. No sense in being like the guy who took a Viagra and had an energy bar and Red Bull before sex, only to drop dead in the shower, as happened to a mutual friend. That was bad enough, but the guy's family blamed her for his death. To add insult to injury, I don't know if they had to worry about rigor mortis setting in.

If it did, what a commercial Pfizer could have on their hands. Regardless, it couldn't help but enhance her reputation as a lethal lover, a genuine femme fatale.

Chapter 6

Word for Cialis

I know a woman, 91, married three times, widowed a few years ago, who is still very attractive, well dressed, always made up, and still sexually active. For the past few years she has had an out-of-state lover, now 96, a classmate from high school or college, whom she has known about 70 years. They get together twice a year, and "get it on," as they say, in CO or FL.

She prefers the latter – fewer distractions, no pets and kids around, and she can have her own bathroom.

Her friends love her and want the best for her, and think she deserves better. The guy thinks she's over-dressed, tries to have her run around in sweats and without makeup, and treats her badly, in their opinion. His only saving grace is that for the first 36 hours after he takes his Cialis, he's a charming stud who can satisfy her every desire. After that, when the Cialis wears off, he's a bastard and treats her poorly.

The sex has been so good that it has overshadowed everything else. Lately, she found that her fake eyelashes have the same effect as Cialis, so he doesn't have to take a pill. She must have a powerful effect on him, at any rate. The first time they got together for a date, he had an erection for three days.

The other day I ran into her by accident at the post office. She was elegantly dressed in a flowered top and white slacks. Her hair was well coiffed and she had her makeup on, along with her fake eyelashes.

When I commented on how beautiful she looked, she winked and said, "I knew I would run into someone I knew if I didn't have my makeup on. That's why I never leave the house without it."

As she headed out the door, two strangers, elderly men she didn't know, fought to open the door for her and to curry her favor.

Recently, we were out to dinner together and someone wanted to take a picture of us together, and I happened to be next to her. So I put my arm around her, and she tilted sideways, turning into and toward me, and I could feel her breast against me, still firm, and I insisted that the photographer take more photos, in case the first one didn't turn out, just so I could feel her pressed against me a little longer.

Sex appeal has no age limit, that's for sure. And neither do lust and horniness.

Chapter

Remaining Faithful

I don't know about Chris, but I find other people attractive. Rarely though, do I have sexual fantasies about beautiful women I see, even though I may openly admire their bodies and their beauty.

Paul Newman said of Joanne Woodward, "Why settle for hamburger when you have steak at home?"

I feel the same way. Except you may be looking at steak, in which case the same logic applies. If you have steak at home, why bother?

If I were attracted to another woman and acted on it, it would speak more about unresolved problems in our relationship and marriage than on the power and suitability of the attraction toward the other woman. It would be a clear signal that there are issues at home that require immediate attention.

So, I don't mind finding other people, especially women, attractive. It suits my appreciation for beauty and aesthetics, and I see no harm in it. At least, that's my rationale.

I take my vows seriously, and put a high priority on loyalty and faithfulness. Not that I'm a goody-goody; I fear the consequences of doing something against my core values, and also, of being caught. Hell hath no fury like a woman catching a hypocrite in the act. I'd rather face a low-carb diet for life than run that risk.

Chapter 8

The Best Part of All

Sex is great, but the best part is going to bed at night and waking up in the morning, turning to the side and wrapping my arms around my wife, pressing her body next to mine until it's like we have just one skin for the both of us.

Her body warmth heats me up and mine heats her up, like one thermostat heating up both of our bodies to the same setting. Covering her lips with many soft kisses is the most exciting, most soothing, most bonding thing to do, and our bodies intuitively react to one another, holding each other as close as we can until we spontaneously have to let go, move back, look at each other, and check to see if it's all real or something we're imagining.

Words seem inadequate then, and we find ourselves saying the same things over and over, little things like:

- "I love you"

- "Thank you"

- "I'm so glad you're in my life"

- "I love you, husband"

- "I love you, wife"

It's a great way to end the day and to start the day, and whatever else that follows is a piece of cake.

Chapter 9

How Much Better Can it Get?

I'm actually still officially on my honeymoon, just two weeks into our marriage. I've been married before, but I don't recall a geometric progression where it gets better and better by the day. It reaches a point where one wonders, Can it get any better than this?

Or, should we slow things down so we don't crash at some point and drop like a rock to a level of mediocrity or boredom?

We get closer in quantum leaps; it's not a steadily growing level of intimacy and togetherness. It's not like a roller coaster ride, because there is no sudden, scary dip like you're going to crash, then feel relieved that you're not.

It's like gasping for air and not being able to breathe, then filling your lungs with fresh air until your chest has doubled in size, then not being able to breathe, letting it all out, then inhaling again until your chest expands even more, filling your lungs past its old capacity, and the cycle begins again and again. I do not comprehend the phenomenon, nor care to.

I'm just along for the ride and enjoying it, staying "in the zone" and feeling blissed out and treating it as if it's normal on one hand, while on the other hand knowing that a miracle is taking place and being fully aware of its awe and splendor.

It's wonderful; life is good, and love is great. The whole world is shiny and clean, and all that's wrong in the world, which fills the newspaper headlines and makes the evening's top news stories, don't touch me. I'm immune from all that.

Chapter 10

Sex Isn't Everything,
But it Might Beat Scrabble

Don't get me wrong. Sex is great, but it's not the number one priority for everybody, especially seniors. Some would rather do without it, do less of it because they're bored with it, it's not as satisfying as it used to be, their libido has severely diminished, they feel "used up," or have a mind-set that they shouldn't put as much focus on it because of their age.

Then again, it is exciting, and even if you love scrabble, it might beat it. The pillow talk before and after is an underrated side benefit. You can talk about how your day went, or just ask idle questions, or make small talk with no particular strategy or agenda in mind.

The fact that you're lying down in a relaxed frame of mind, in an environment where you're not likely to be disturbed or interrupted, creates an intimacy where bonding is enhanced. The physical fact that you are closer and sharing intimacies makes you emotionally closer, and invites more intimacies. You don't even have to have sex, although it's likely to occur. The snuggling, nuzzling, hugging, kissing, holding each other is warm and wonderful, giving you the fuzzy wuzzies and a feeling of bliss. That is hard to beat. And the more you find it enjoyable, the more likely you'll want to do it over and over again.

Chemically speaking, you may be talking clinically about oxytocin and endorphins, but romantically speaking, you're talking about that wonderful feeling called love:

- Why people gravitate to each other

- Why they marry

- Why they want to be together for the rest of their lives

- What makes the world go around

- What gives a halo effect to your life

I'm not saying to throw out the scrabble board. Keep it, but there's more entertainment available than you can find in the TV Guide.

Chapter 11

3 PM Friday Matinees

We are Equal Time Practitioners, and do not discriminate against time. We have done it at bedtime, which is usually around 10 PM, and at midnight, and at 2 AM, 3 AM, 4 AM and 5 AM (not always on the same night), but we had an especially memorable time one Friday afternoon, at 3 PM, which we called a matinee session.

I don't recall the particulars, unfortunately, and don't recall doing anything different, and don't recall having eaten or drunk anything out of the ordinary, so it must have been the mood, the timing, our appetite, the luck of execution, and the serendipity accident of physical and emotional congruence.

Whatever the cause, the results were spectacular and extraordinary, and like Linda Lovelace's directorial picture effects when she had her orgasms in "Deep Throat," there were fireworks, rockets bursting, church bells ringing, and the ground under us seemed to have a shifting of tectonic plates.

While it was very recent, we hope to pursue continuing research on the matter and hope to simulate and replicate the conditions and create the same effects. After gathering a sufficient number of clinical trials for an adequate sampling, we will report back on the matter if we come across any substantive related conditions and factors.

While it might be of interest, anecdotal reports offer no scientific validation as would the reliability of quantitative cause-and-effect data. It may take some time to set up the appropriate paradigm and descriptor parameters, but we are in no hurry to rush to judgment or conjecture in this dynamic behavioral matter.

Our decision may be somewhat arbitrary, but to honor the authenticity and structural integrity of the data, our research-gathering will be done only on Fridays at 3 PM. This limited sampling may take six months to a year, which will provide a small universe of only 26 to 52, so we are contemplating a 2-year study so the sampling will exceed 100.

A potentially offsetting factor is that by that time, we could hardly call ourselves honeymooners, which could see a diminution in our marital ardor. A possible consideration is for us to increase the frequency of incidence from once to twice a session, where we compound the complexity of the control factors in that there may be a diminution of energy and enthusiasm, potentially offset by an improvement in performance and heightened desire and pleasure due to "finding the groove" or falling into a rhythm or being in a zone.

Other follow-up studies that suggest academic interest are the effect of matinees on evening encounters (technically, post-bedtime, including those after midnight), whether they affect frequency and quality of enjoyment.

All of the preceding suggest that we have barely seen the tip of the iceberg, and there is much more that we could explore and learn from.

Footnote: More than two months later, for various reasons, we have not adhered to our Friday matinee schedule. Instead, we have fallen into the habit of enjoying early morning specials at various times after midnight, 3:30, 5:00 and 6:00 being the most popular, with equally spectacular success. This has shortened my CPAP-wearing sleep, my mask I wear for sleep apnea, since I take it off as it impedes sexual activity. Not to be graphic, but imagine kissing someone who's wearing a diving mask, and you'll get the picture.

Chapter 12

Learn from Astrology about Sex

Mea culpa, that's a cheap trick to get your attention. I don't know anything about astrology, and know very little about sex, but since both are intriguing topics that easily capture the attention of many people, putting the two words together has a synergistic impact of increasing your target audience without much effort.

I picked up my wife's astrology magazine because she wanted me to read an "interesting" article on the current state of world events, as viewed by an astrologer, and how astrology could be used as a synthesizing tool, a prism, if you will, so you can look at an otherwise-complicated seemingly unrelated series of events and be able to see the totality of the mosaic, the holistic view, of an era or significant period in a single snapshot.

The magazine had individual words that I recognized but which, when used together, had absolutely no meaning for me. I may as well have been looking at hieroglyphics in a cave and tried to interpret the story of what was being depicted. "Neptune In Pisces…Lunar Cycles… The Uranus-Plato Years" and the subject article, "Revolutions and Revelations: An Interview with Jessica Murray" were some of the words I tried to translate into some coherent meaning.

Ms. Murray is an articulate 60-year-old woman who is clearly intelligent, with a wide grasp of a number of current events, and able to interpret what she has gone through for the last 40 years or so, including her SDS, McGovern, social activism and hippie days, her growth in the field of astrology, and how she used the latter to see thematic patterns in her life. I found her brilliant and articulate, and didn't have a clue what she was saying.

Sex is the same thing to me. I hear words that I think I understand, and when grouped together I can make a stab at what they're talking about, but on closer examination, I find myself on shaky ground.

- What is a man?

- What is a woman?

- How are they alike?

- How do they differ?

A very long time ago, I guess philosophers and priests could address those questions with some self-proclaimed degree of authority, but in later years, psychologists and psychiatrists seem to have taken on that role, and speak knowingly and write books that explain such mysteries as why men have nipples, why men don't listen and why women can't read maps, and why women can multi-task but why men cannot.

In today's age, we want instant gratification. When it comes to information, we are blessed with the Internet, Google and Wikipedia, and can find out about just about everything. But while we may be able to get millions of hits on the subject, I'm not sure that we can get a comprehensive, in-depth answer to the same basic questions I raised about men, women and sex in general.

We do process information based on our biases and what we already believe, and tend to put more confidence into something that says what we're already predisposed to believe, and tend to dismiss as not true those things that are not consistent with what we already believe. Pragmatically, that's why we can turn to our horoscope, our favorite psychologist or general columnist, to see what they say go guide us through the day or our current crisis or dilemma, select what seems to make the most sense to us at that moment, and go on from there.

And if that advice or information doesn't turn out to be relevant or accurate, most of us shrug it off and somehow make it our fault, as if we were an exception to the situation being discussed, or we misinterpreted what we read, or whatever.

Which is another way of saying, when it comes to sex, I may as well look up my horoscope, natal chart, sun chart, and follow how the planets are aligned for that day. I'd have an even-money chance of being right compared to my using my intellect, knowledge and background to make a sexual assessment and decision.

Chapter 13

Effects of Porn Flicks on Eating Healthy

In the interest of continuing self-growth and enjoying an improved sex life, we studiously watched some porn flicks the other afternoon. One of them, "The Devil In Miss Jones," starring Georgina Spelvin, had a reverse effect on our health beliefs; we grew up thinking that eating fruits was healthy and is good for us.

In one of the scenes, the star is reclining nude in bed with a large bowl of fruit. She literally licks her chops while savoring an apple, then rubs it against her vagina, and while we were gasping and fearing that she would swallow it, she brought it to her lips and took a lingering, lusty bite out of it.

Then she picked up a bunch of grapes (seedless, I hope), plucked them one by one, and inserted them into her body orifice, storing them for a later snack. Then she plucked a banana, rubbed it with her fingers suggestively, then inserted it slowly into herself, pulled it out, then peeled it, then ate it slowly.

Still hungry, she searched into her grape bag and plucked out the grapes, one at a time, eating them with much gusto.

I understand that fruits are a good source of vitamins and nutrients, and are best eaten fresh, and that one should eat several servings a day for optimal health. But I'll never be able to see a grape, banana or apple in the same way henceforth, and may prefer to puree them, or put them in a blender and have a smoothie instead.

My sweet, innocent wife, who was raised a Catholic in Milwaukee, shocked me when she said, "I know that name from some place, Georgina Spelvin. How do I know her?"

Spelvin looked like she was in her late 20s, early 30s, and the film was made in 1979, putting her in her early 50s to early 60s. I did not want to know the answer, so I didn't help her to refresh her memory, where she might have known of Ms. Spelvin.

Chapter 14

Keeping it in the Family

My wife has two pet dogs, Remus and Allie, who are part of the family. Remus is a red heeler, a brown-and-white cattle dog, about 55 pounds, wiry and all muscle, and 5 years old. He is easier to manage and well behaved, and has the art of begging down to a science, not being obnoxious or obvious, but very close at hand, looking up with soulful eyes and alert for any scrap that might fall to the floor.

Chris picked him up in Arkansas at a yard sale. Allie, a spirited 3, is part black Lab, part Weimaraner, with sleek black fur that glistens, and golden eyes, and weighing 58 pounds. She belonged to Paul, Chris' oldest son who lives in Rogers, Arkansas. She was crated up almost all day because both owners worked. As a result, Allie was almost impossible to handle when Chris took Allie off their hands. Though much better now, she still bolts out of the garage door when it opens, and we have to go after her in the car, taking five to 30 minutes to hunt her down and bring her home. She also has separation anxiety, chewing up books or DVDs if we are away from the house too long, so we usually put her in her wire crate when we leave the house for any length of time.

They both rule the roost at home, sleeping on whatever sofa or bed is handy, and we usually have to chase them off the bed at night. They wake us up in the morning, starting from 5 o'clock, wanting to be let out to relieve themselves or to have an early morning romp in the back yard, or wanting to be fed.

Sometimes, in the early morning, we find ourselves wanting to make love just before the dogs wake up, and as you can imagine, we kick off the covers and get tangled up in the sheets, sometimes lying naked in bed. And just about that time, we hear them arise from their dog beds set alongside the closet with sliding panels, shake their fur and rattle their collars, much like a human stretching on his toes and yawning when he arises.

We try to ignore them, not wanting to be distracted from the throes of sexual play, and I often find my limbs stretched out, one arm or one leg dangling over the side of the bed, and invariably that's the moment that Allie puts her front paws onto the bed, wanting to get us out of the bed, and wanting, demanding that I pet her as she licks my hand, leg or face, whatever she can reach.

Remus is more aggressive and hops onto the bed and lies down next to one of us, snuggling up and pressing his side against our body.

It feels like we're having an orgy, in bed with another couple; while holding Chris and kissing her, I'm petting Allie with one hand, and on the other side of the bed, I can feel Remus leaning his body into ours, wanting some of the action.

Both have been fixed and I'm sure there are no sexual undertones for them as they join us in bed, but it does give me an odd sensation, pressing the soft naked skin on one side and stroking Allie's or Remus' fur with another hand. I sigh and figure it's all in the family, so it should be all right, but enough is enough. It's hard to continue to be sexually intimate with a human partner when, six inches from your face, you look up and see two friendly eyes quietly observing what you're doing.

At that point, Chris usually gives me a last, long kiss, gets up, gets dressed, and lets the dogs out into the back yard, head for the kitchen to feed them, and to start another wonderful day.

Chapter 15

Sex and Golf; Alike and Different

I'm passionate about both. I'm not particularly skillful at either, but that doesn't stop me from really enjoying both activities, and partaking at both every chance I get. However, in golf, I'm not particular whom I'm paired up with.

I prefer those who are friendly, positive, love the game, and care more about enjoying themselves than how well their game goes or how well they do. I really don't care if they lie or cheat (unless we're playing for money, even for small stakes), because I'm not competing with them but against myself and my standards and expectations, the course, and not so much against par.

In sex, I'd rather play with the same partner and don't like to play **shotgun** or **scramble**. In both, you can choose to engage in **match play** or **stroke play**. In sex, you can choose either type of play. **Match play** is for the more serious-minded who focus more on relationships; they want a good match, whether it's for a marriage or for a life partner or steady boyfriend or girlfriend.

Stroke play is more about sex, as the name implies.

In golf, in match play, you're playing for "*skins*," which can be confusing in that sex is usually but not limited to being in "*skins*." In golf, the object of the game is to go around in the fewest strokes possible. In sex, usually, partners prefer to take the maximum number of strokes. In golf, players usually play 9 or 18 holes and a hole-in-one is a rarity.

In sex, the latter is quite common, and players usually prefer to play only one hole, although some adventurous types play with one or two other holes.

At the end of a round, golfers usually celebrate at the 19th hole, where they drink, lie and boast about their exploits, often at the expense of others. And the winner usually buys the drinks, which are almost like a sacrament.

By comparison, with sex, drinking, if at all applicable, takes place before, not after sex. In golf, some players actually drink during the round. Some think that it actually enhances their performance, while others don't really care, they just enjoy drinking.

And it would be in extremely bad form to belittle the other person after sex, even in jest, and to poke fun at their flubs and mistakes. Ironically, in golf, it seems to enrich the game just played and to motivate the players to get together soon to do it again, with the good-natured threat that next time, they will turn the tables on them and beat them badly.

That certainly would not be welcome in sex, and would not inspire a return engagement.

Both activities can be sources of addiction, fascination, frustration, humility, humiliation, and an infinite number of outcomes, hence the high interest in both forms of presumed pleasure. Although the players may not reach the desired outcomes always, the journey seems to be more important than the destination.

And although they will never know perfection nor master either, the participants appear committed to both and it is highly unlikely that they will give up on either. Just ask someone who has had a terrible experience if they are available to do it again next week, and in most cases, they will say "yes" enthusiastically, and ask, "What time and where?"

Chapter 16

A "Minor" Misunderstanding

Misunderstandings occur in all relationships. They are a natural part of the relationship.

Some blow over, some do not; some escalate, some fester, and some create distance and demilitarized zones where the couple do not go back to, or tread very lightly when they try to feel their way through this discomfort. It takes patience and effective communication skills to walk through the minefield, especially when feelings are already hurt and one or both are defensive and guarded.

When they occur, they never feel "minor" and feel like there's a serious, perhaps permanent rift in the relationship, and it feels like you may never again have a normal conversation.

Minor Misunderstanding
The usual pattern is:

1. *Abe says something*.

2. *Jane says something back*, or nothing, when
a desired response is expected. There is a
disconnect, a miscommunication, a perceived
slight or intentional hurt on the part of Abe.

3. If Jane is unaware of the miscommunication or
perceived slight or hurt, *Abe gets infuriated*,
angry, upset, self-righteous, indignant. Abe
freezes up, withdraws into a shell, lashes out
verbally, flees physically, or may cry. The verbal
reaction of Abe to Jane, may be coming out of left
field, like in an equation where $1 + 2 =$ longitude
21 degrees, latitude 90 degrees, 9 am Greenwich
Time.

4. If Abe doesn't say anything and it gets suddenly
deathly quiet, *Jane will sense* that something
is wrong but doesn't know what it is. If they
are in bed kissing, Abe may tentatively return
a kiss, then pause, waiting for Jane to say or do
the "right" thing to indicate remorse or offer an
apology or some form of reassurance. All of this is
non-verbally communicated, so if Jane doesn't get
it, he's in deep trouble.

5. Sometimes Jane may say something *insensitive
or stupid*, sometimes it's simply taken the wrong

way. But if Jane is tired and is not mentally sharp or tuned in to the shifting nuances in the nurturing or loving mode of their relationship, things usually escalate and the functionally effective nature of their relationship will likely deteriorate.

At this point, it's a *Chinese fire drill*, combined with the smooth efforts of passengers trying to get out of an airplane when the engines have sputtered and died down, and you can feel the plane going down. You know it's foolhardy to jump out, but you know it's fatal if you stay in the plane, and that either way, you are in deep trouble.

6. If *Abe leaves* the bed and the room, you know he will never come back and you wonder about such things as, I have only one suitcase: What do I pack? It's impossible to go back to sleep, and you're afraid to go to her, imagining she's probably still fuming and angry, and there'll be an ugly scene, and you'll be yelling at each other without knowing what the argument is all about.

Abe will be referring to one thing and Jane will be talking about something else, and neither will know what the other is talking about. So you stay in bed, keeping your eyes closed and trying to sleep, while the adrenaline is pumping like mad and your breath is still coming in short gasps.

7. Somehow, the ***madness subsides***, Abe returns to bed, nothing is said, and the silent reconciliation takes place, sometimes distracted by sex in desperation, as if it could undo whatever has happened. Then the breathing returns in deep, even exhalations and inhalations, you cling to each other until sleep overtakes you, and one or the other will bring it up later in the morning, or in the day, and life returns to normal – hopefully.

Chapter 17

The Eleventh Commandment

Before anyone decides to write a book, he should ascertain that he knows a bit more than the average reader about the subject. In looking at where I am in this book, seventeen chapters in only about twenty pages of actual writing, the amount of my ignorance is indeed staggering and humbling. The average informed writer could probably write twenty pages in a single chapter covering just one topic, and not be satisfied in basically writing a blog for seventeen times.

Having said that, he shouldn't ramble on and on to stretch a point. He should say what he has to say, and stop.

Chapter 18

Breaking The Primary Rule

At the risk of incurring the wrath and jealousy of my wife Chris, who considers Sally her soul sister, hiking partner and dear friend, I freely admit to finding Sally warm, charismatic, positive, friendly, radiant, and attractive beyond her physical beauty. She is as irresistible as a puppy, the picture of good health (despite her many ailments), a striking contrast with her deep, dark tan and short, white hair, dazzling smile and commercial-white teeth.

She is the friend that every woman wants, the woman that every man wants. Yet she is loyal to her friends, ethical, plays by the rules, and does not poach. She is kind and courteous, generous with her praise, and shows her love for one and all in the spirit of agape.

She is also an enigma. While she claims she wants to fall in love again, she continues to wear what looks like her wedding ring on her left hand, which would seem to tell any male that she is married and not available. It has been six years since her 20-year marriage ended, her heart broken by deceit and betrayal at the hands of a man she claims she has forgiven, and still loves. Perhaps she loves him still, not in the all-forgiving way, but as a hurt wife, even though he has remarried, to a woman he met while on their 20th anniversary trip to Hawaii.

Her commitment to her friends runs deep; she took care of an ailing friend, caring for him for three months while he was in critical care in Ohio hospitals. She herself collapsed and had to be hospitalized, spending a few months recovering in Denver and forgoing her doctor's recommendation that she get a pacemaker.

She is going to Brasilia in a week from tomorrow, to receive healing from John of God. Though her medical ailments run seven single-spaced pages, and she was told last week that she might lose sight of her right eye, heading her list of priorities are two things: to restore her vision, and to know God. She might be talked into adding her immune system, which is probably the linchpin for her lupus, Epstein-Barr, connective tissue issues and other disorders which have already cost her hip replacements and a bad knee.

We'll be praying for her, and know that John of God and the entities he incorporates will address her main health needs. It will take a lot of entities to keep her in check when she regains her health, and is able to do everything she wants to do, but can't now.

Chapter 19

Health and High Altitude

Sedona is roughly 5,500 feet above sea level, whereas Hawaii is just about at sea level. Ever since I moved to Sedona, I have felt the thin air affecting me at the driving range.

In Hawaii, while I would stop and take a break to contemplate why I was going left or right or hitting bad shots, though a bit tired, I wasn't short of breath. In Arizona, even at 3,300 feet above sea level at Verde Santa Fe driving range, I do get tired and winded, and find it necessary to stop and catch my breath. During the few times that I've played here in Arizona, I've used a riding cart and haven't gotten winded, and after the round I'm feeling fine.

I lived in Hawaii for many years, but sex never got me gasping for air and out of breath the way it affects me now, in Arizona. So, definitely, the thin air does make a difference; I'm also more tired, generally, suggesting that it might affect my hypertension medicines.

Two things come to mind: one, my dosage may have to be adjusted to account for the thinner air so I won't get out of breath as fast or as often. Second, sex with my wife is a quantum leap from what I was accustomed to, and it is so exciting and draws so much more energy out of me, that it/she causes me to be out of air and breathless, and/or my fitness and conditioning have deteriorated so rapidly that it is causing these respiratory responses.

It sounds like a pleasant enough problem, but it does raise a question whether my health is at issue, or I'm just married to an incredible sex goddess whose impact on me may be more than I can physically handle. At any rate, she says she wants me to stick around for a long while, and doesn't want to have to explain to paramedics why and how I suddenly stopped breathing in bed. She would rather not have to explain in detail the activities that we were engaged in prior to their arrival.

The prudent thing to do is to get a second medical opinion on the dosage of my medication, which I'll do in a month to see if I've acclimated to the Arizona air. Empirically, since we're going back to Hawaii in late August for my late mother's memorial service, that would be a good way to compare notes, to see how I react to sex in Hawaii.

I could see no change, get worse or get better. If I see no change, it would suggest that my sex partner is the primary cause for my getting short of breath, assuming we stay with the same sexual positions that we have been using. If I get worse, it suggests that my sex partner is even more powerful in Hawaii, and that the Hawaiian atmosphere that I've been accustomed to has relaxed me and allowed me to enjoy sex even more, but that my general fitness has not kept pace with the physical requirements of our sexual proclivities.

And if I feel better, it would suggest that the thinner Arizona air was the primary factor, which may or may not influence a move back to Hawaii. They say that sex and money are two main stress factors in marriage, and I'd hate to have to choose between sex and money and how it might affect our marriage. I'd rather enjoy the sex and the marriage regardless of how breathless or how exhausted I get. And if that should be a bad choice health-wise, what a way to go.

Chapter 20

Sex and Sally, Amanda, Chris and Me

Last night we had two friends over for dinner that I'll call Sally and Amanda. We had one of my favorite things that Chris makes, fish tacos. Simple but delicious – a sauce for the fish sticks made with yogurt, mayonnaise and some other ingredients, a salsa with tomatoes, cilantro, onions, habanero or chili pepper and some other goodies, cabbage, and flour and corn tortillas.

None of us were drinking, so we were all sober but the conversation was free-flowing and uninhibited, as it is with close friends you don't have to impress or put up a front for.

For some reason the subject turned to sex – when we first had sex, and what ensued. Sally's story is best, so I'll tell hers. She was a senior in high school and was curious about it, and wanted to try it with her boyfriend. She confided in a girlfriend, who had already had sex for the first time a year earlier. After her date, her girl friend asked, "Well? Did you do it?"

Sally looked confused and said, "Sorta, kinda."

Her friend said, "What do you mean? You either did it or you didn't. Tell me exactly what happened."

After Sally explained, the girl friend said, "You did it, no question."

Sally exploded, "What's the big deal? I have more fun roasting marshmallows!"

She has a bad heart condition and had to go to ER the night before, with a blood pressure reading of 80 over 30 with a pulse of 48. She had hosted a party at her home and could hardly breathe, and felt that her chest was being crushed. The nurses told her that her heart was not in a good condition, and that she should see a cardiologist immediately.

When we found out, we scolded her and ordered her to see a cardiologist first thing in the morning. Chris advised her to whine and complain and to report her readings, that she felt faint, and would die unless she saw a cardiologist immediately.

Amanda chimed in and read her the riot act, told her in no uncertain terms that she had better call the cardiologist first thing in the morning, and to call her to let her know that she had an appointment. Chris volunteered to drive her to the doctor's.

Feeling uncomfortable by all this attention, Sally tried to change the subject and said, she met a very good looking guy, about ten years younger who wants to take her on a date. She said she had some things to do and a trip to make, but would give him a call as soon as she came back. She asked us if she should see him.

When she told us his name, Amanda said, "Clint? I know him. He is very good looking, but last I heard he's married."

Sally said, "He told me he's single, and has no children."

Amanda said, "And he has some kids."

We chatted some more, and discovered they were talking about two different Clints, so Sally sighed with relief.

"Maybe he won't want to go out with me when he finds out I have a serious heart problem."

She reconsidered, "But I could kick up my pacemaker so we could have sex, as long as I don't drop dead on him."

Amanda announced that she was going on a date tomorrow with another shuttle worker for another company. Since he lives in Sun City West and she in Sedona, and they only would meet by accident when they were at the same layover spots sporadically, they were going to meet at Black Canyon City, more or less a mid-point place for a rendezvous.

Amanda has reservations since it sounded like he's still married, although he says he's divorced, and he may just be looking for a way to stay in the States since he's Canadian.

She finds him sweet but there's no chemistry; he's overweight and crass, with such endearing things to say as, "I had dreams about you last night" and flowery, gushy things and wanting to make out in the back seat of either of their trolleys. She said she prefers a bed, and wasn't agile enough to make out in the back seat of a car. We could picture her lifting up her legs halfway into the air to demonstrate her loss of flexibility.

Sally suggested she should first ask for his medical records before going out on a date with him, perhaps in light of her own medical history. Amanda said, "He does have Crohn's Disease."

Sally suggested, "You'd better get on top, otherwise he might get diarrhea all over you."

She also suggested, "And you might hold your arms over your head and grab the headboard. Or keep the lights out if you get on top, because you don't want him to see if your breasts are sagging."

I suggested, "You can just fling them over your shoulders."

Chris also recounted her days as a psychiatric nurse in Mystic, CT, when she saw one of another nurse's charges, Lily Ann, an obese, black woman with huge boobs, walk around with a see-through top with no bra. She advised the other nurse to tell Lily Ann to change into something more appropriate, and the nurse replied, "Not me! You tell her."

Lily Ann also had a violent temper, and could deck any hospital orderly or nurse, and everyone gave her a wide berth.

Chris also remembered a tall, thin nurse who used to wear colorful bikinis under her white uniform in those days when miniskirts were in fashion, and when she walked down the hall, everyone could see her bikinis.

Amanda chimed in about an elementary school teacher of her son when he was about six, who wore miniskirts and garter belts that would show whenever she would bend over to pick up something. Amanda was mortified that six-year-olds should see something like that.

We laughed so hard throughout the evening that there were times that no one spoke. There were just rolls of laughter, one laugh evoking the rest of us to laugh, or to come up with another funny add-on line to expand on a funny scenario. It was one of the most laugh-filled evenings we have had.

Chapter 21

The Virtues of Being Married

Last night, around eight o'clock, my wife thoughtfully brought to me as I was working on my laptop a glass of water and a Viagra pill, in case I would forget to take it an hour ahead of bedtime, which I had been prone to do lately. I finished what I was doing and joined her in the living room to watch TV for an hour before we normally retired, around ten o'clock.

I had played 18 holes of golf earlier in the day, had shot a miserable 104, the last of about eight in the past two months, and was totally distracted by the sad state of my golfing, and was in no mood for sex.

On top of that, I was a bit tired, perhaps from mental exhaustion as I tried to figure out if my bad golf was due to bad fundamental mechanics, a poor mental game, or both, if one was a bigger problem than the other, and if one exacerbated the other. I wondered if I should return to lessons and be under the watchful eye of a Class A teaching pro, who could spot in an instant what was wrong and give me the magic formula, the secret key, and elevate me to the single-digit status that I thought I so richly deserved. Shooting in the mid 90s and low 100s for nearly three months was not my idea of the kind of golf I thought I was capable of playing.

When we got into bed, instead of snuggling and kissing and warming up for some marital sex, I held her close as we usually do but I vented to her about my golfing woes and that I might need to take some golfing lessons to get a handle on my problems on the course, and to figure out if my mental game was responsible for my swing breakdowns, or if my swing breakdowns were due to lack of focus and worsening my mental game, resulting in a snowball of double bogeys and triple bogeys. She would occasionally turn my head and kiss me and try to turn my focus back to my marital duties, but to no avail; I apologized and told her I was tired, and would have to back out of my conjugal duties as a husband.

She replied, "Too bad you didn't tell me before taking the Viagra," implying it would be a waste of $22. At that ghastly price, it's like flushing money down the toilet. She said something about, "there's always tomorrow," and let me go off to sleep.

Much later, after going to the bathroom, around 6 AM, my hormones must have been stirring or the

Viagra had a longer potency effect than advertised, or as I told my wife, she could get my motor going even if I didn't take a Viagra, because she was the greatest answer to ED, stronger than any blue pill. We made great love, "The best, Class A Number One," as I told her.

Later in the morning, as we were driving to her golf lesson, I thanked her for being patient and understanding and for not getting upset about the night before. She said that we're married and retired, and in no rush, and there's always another day, and a few hours won't make a difference. What a sweetheart.

That, I think, is a great advantage in being married, and in being retired; we don't have to do anything on a certain day or a certain hour (except for medical appointments and social engagements, which are still a matter of choice), and can choose to make love at ten in the morning or 3:30 AM or 6 AM or 3 PM on a Friday afternoon, have to reach an agreement only with ourselves, and often it's an unplanned, spontaneous thing.

I don't know what other married couples in their 70s, or newlyweds, no matter how old or young they are, do things, but I doubt if there are many couples, married or otherwise, young or old, who lie in bed in each other's arms, and talk about golf and how much of it is mental and how much is mechanical, and how much is concentration and how much is talent.

We conjectured what Heather, Chris' teaching pro, might tell me, like:

- "Tell you what – give it up"

- "It looks like LOFT
  – Lack Of Friggin' Talent"

- "Keep at it and don't give up"

- "You'll get it one of these days."

I told Chris I would take a lesson with Heather as well, and that I had decided to take five ½ hour sessions with her. I'll be taking my first lesson with her at 5:30 PM today. Heather is an excellent teacher; I learned quite a few things from her, mainly, to chip with a 7, 8 or 9 iron from within ten yards of the green, a hybrid or a putter from just off the green, and NOT use a pitching wedge or sand wedge from within 10 yards, which has been my practice. She also caught me cheating, turning my head and looking at the ball when chipping instead of keeping my head down for a three-second count before looking at the ball.

What was promising was that she watched me chip and said I should be a single-digit golfer. What a great judge of talent!

Chapter 22

Size Does Matter

Some things don't change and are immutable: death, taxes, and penis envy. My wife Chris, an avid student of Egyptology who has been to Egypt twice, saw in Milwaukee Museum the mummified remains of a diminutive Egyptian king. Laying flaccid to one side was an 8" penis. With another king, his erect penis was appropriately wrapped for the occasion; it was also disproportionately large for his stature.

According to some reports, when thieves came upon the mummy of King Tutankhamen, they broke his arms and fingers to remove his jewelry and pectorals. They must have been impressed with the size of his penis because they broke it off and took it, and it has never been recovered.

In modern porn flicks and in ED ads, if you were to judge the size of men's penises (penii?) by what you see portrayed, 9 out of 10 men would cover their crotches in shame and humiliation for falling far short of the mark. The typical model in these media is so well-endowed that the women can wrap both hands around the penis and still not cover the entire subject.

So what can the average male, especially a shriveled senior, do about it to enhance his masculinity?

One quick and harmless way is to clip the pubic hair (and pluck the white ones) so it appears there's more than meets the eye, like a truck in a side view mirror appearing larger than it is.

Others could try stretching exercises or suction pumps, but I'm not into exercise and am not mechanically inclined. A third alternative is to sort out the ED literature that most seniors are deluged with, and to try some of the pills and potions, lotions and patches that promise you instant growth and rock-hard erections. I've tried a few of them – well, actually, a LOT of them, such as Irexis, Testo24, Oliorix, Instamax and many others that I threw out whose names I don't recall, and they didn't help at all. I can say the same for Viagra, Cialis and Levitra, the Big Three of Senior Pharma, and they all fell flatter than my sought-after erection.

Taking hypertension meds doesn't help the cause one bit. If Pfizer could develop a hypertension drug that would not only prevent impotency but enhance erections, they would surpass Salk for his fight against polio and amass even more obscene fortunes than they now garner.

Despite the widespread belief, use it or lose it, celibacy – voluntary, forced or otherwise , does not cause the penis to atrophy. And, despite the secretive popularity of masturbation, even among married people, it does not enhance the size of the penis, no matter how hard you tug and pull. Like golf, where most men play even though they don't get any better, I don't see any decline in the behind-the-bathroom-door popularity of masturbation among men.

I personally have no knowledge about the incidence of masturbation among women and can't comment on it. Despite the seeming propensity of women to do it in porn flicks, I would guess it's not as common among women as it is with men.

To clarify all of the above, size does matter, up to a point. To reassure us "smaller" guys, bigger is not always better. A guy who is too well-hung could cause not only discomfort but pain to the woman. It's not a battering or bludgeoning contest, and there's much to be said for skill, sensitivity, awareness of your partner's preferences and "choice" spots.

In other words, it's what you do with what you've got, not the number of inches you pack or comparability to rock or steel. I take comfort in that

I've never caused any pain to my wife because I'm too large or so hard that I feel like a steel piston chiseling through rock.

Chapter 23

A Position Statement

I should admit up front that I have the Kama Sutra but have never read it or tried to follow it. I also have such savory titles as Sexual Secrets and How To Give Her An Orgasm In Thirty Seconds, and have read about the nuances of a clitoral orgasm versus a G-Spot orgasm, but have never mastered these subtleties.

I'm grateful I can find the appropriate opening to find my way in, and don't have the know-how to look at special nooks and crannies like the clitoris and G-Spot.

Besides, it would be hard for me to act and feel natural during sex with an open book that I hold with one hand, held behind her back, with a coal miner's lamp or flashlight in my mouth so I can read the text and see the illustrations on some esoteric position I want to try.

I stumbled upon something that works quite well

for us. When we go to bed at night, she holds up the bed sheets for me as I slip into bed, and as we snuggle to say good night, that's one of the best times of the day for us. We can talk about what happened in the day or what we're going to do the next day, engaging in pillow talk and warmed up by each other's bodies, and the mere closeness to your loved one induces snuggling, coziness, kissing and fondling, and we wrap each other's legs around each other, and next thing you know, we come across some novel and imaginative ways to cohabit.

I'm not sure if they are covered in the sex manuals like the Kama Sutra, but I would wager that we have come across some positions that are not even listed in the index or covered in any chapter.

The other night we even tried something new for us, very fresh and innovative, and it turned out to be the missionary position. We had been using so many different positions that it was a rare treat to be trying something that most people would find mundane, ordinary and boring.

I'm all for throwing out the book and the coal miner's head lamp and winging it, and relying on letting nature take its course.

Chapter 24

Erectile Dysfunction and Other Myths

I've mentioned the various things I've tried in the last chapter, so I won't repeat them here. Ever since I had a couple of strokes in 1998, the hypertension medication that my doctor at Kaiser put me on caused overnight impotency. It was disastrous at the time because I was in a relationship, but as luck would have it, she went on Lexapro shortly after that (an anti-depressant), and it did to her libido what my hypertension medication did to my potency.

She lost interest in sex and I couldn't get it up, so it was a miracle that we stayed together for two or three years after that. I then went celibate for about ten years, until I remarried a few months ago, and it was amazing that I didn't need a 3-in-1 oil or WD 40 can before having sex for the first time in ten years. If I could have ejaculated, I'm sure that rust would have come out.

I have found that the best aphrodisiac for an ED

sufferer is a loving wife. It helps if she's also lustful and has a healthy appetite for sex. I lucked out in that she loves me as much as I love her, and I was amazed to find out that even if I can't get a hard erection and it's as hard as a marshmallow, love (or sex) finds a way, and it hasn't been a problem for us, proving that love is the best aphrodisiac.

The upside is that I spend more time on foreplay, for a LONG time, kissing and fondling and enjoying oral sex, so that even before penetration, she's already nearly satiated. I say nearly, not quite, but the senses are heightened and each thrust or grind elicits moans of joy.

Maybe it's out of gratitude more than sensual arousal that at least I got it to half-mast and got it in, but she seems to enjoy our sex. Whenever I apologize for my soft-hearted status, her ego-boosting reply is, "You don't hear me whining and complaining, do you?"

How can you not love a wife like that?

Same thing with *the size* of my penis. Whenever I make disparaging remarks about it --Sorry, Wee Willie seems to be still sleeping--she reassures me my size (or lack of it) is not a problem, and says, "If you were a half-inch bigger, I'd have a real problem with you." Makes me feel like a John Holmes.

Another myth I'd like to shatter is the *efficacy*

of pheromones. According to the ads, one whiff of it and any woman within ten feet of you will be irresistibly drawn to you an will do everything in her power to seduce you on the spot, even in public, whether they know you or not, whether they're married or going with someone else or not, whether they find you physically attractive or not. I tried them, and it had no noticeable effect.

What I found the most effective is my wife's favorite cologne for me, Jaipur, and I spray it on around my neck, the back of my neck and below the navel, and she's all over me like a lion jumping on raw meat.

Chapter 25

Husband's Life on a Short Leash

We have two dogs, Allie and Remus, that take us for morning and evening walks. Actually, Chris usually takes them out in the morning, and I usually join them for the evening walk. I usually have Remus, a red heeler (a cattle dog), and she usually has Allie, a Black Lab – Weimaraner who is a bolter and loves to run after rabbits.

Remus likes to be the alpha dog and tugs at the leash trying to get me to go faster or go left instead of right. I have to rein him in to slow him down to my slower speed, so I find it easier to wrap the leash around my hand so she's on a short leash and I can have better control of him.

You would think that a wise wife would keep her husband on a long leash to give him the illusion of maximum freedom, but most of the wives I know and met prefer to use a short leash.

Friends of ours were joking around the other day

and it prompted my wife Chris to say that she should write a book, 'How To Raise A Husband'. I pre-empted her by writing this chapter, and it appears, empirically, that she deploys a short leash on me.

I disagree with that and want to assert my individuality and rights as a free husband (an oxymoron?). I will always get the last word in and win every argument, no two ways about it. It may be a pyrrhic victory, however, in that my last words are "Yes, dear," or "Whatever you say, dear."

PS My wife just read this and says that I should say that she feels the only way to raise a husband is on a short leash but spoil him rotten; when he's gasping with passion, he'll do anything she wants him to do.

Chapter 26

My Last Willie and Testament

I guess every couple uses a euphemism or nickname for his penis. I never hear anyone call it Johnson; others who are crass may simply call it prick or dick. We're probably on the cute side by calling it willie. I tried the more formal William, Will, and the nickname Bill, but they just don't sound right.

It leads to all kinds of puns and inside jokes – will power, will I or won't, I have the willienillies, gee williekers, and the like. When I die, I haven't decided it I want to be cremated and have my ashes scattered, along with those of Tadashi and Freckles, Chris' dogs who died and whose ashes are in the living room cabinet.

Since Chris is an Egyptophile, I could have mine cut off and preserved for her to keep on her mantel, but willie is so small that I'd have to get as much of an erection as I can before having it cut off, and how do I figure out the logistics since I probably won't have much warning before I die. Or, I could rely on rigor mortis, hoping I'd die in bed while in the middle of sex. If it were in a flaccid state, I imagine she could keep it under glass, like a ball with the falling snowflakes when you shake it, or maybe under two small sheets of glass or laminate, like a pressed leaf. It wouldn't take much space, and she could use it as a paper weight on her desk.

I'd have to give Chris verbal instructions beforehand and she'd have to take care of matters herself, before the paramedics or coroner arrives. If she had to have the will read and executed, too much time will have elapsed, and in this situation, action has to betaken while the iron is hot, or, to be more explicit, while the willie is reasonably hard.

Painful as it sounds, since I'd be dead anyway, I won't feel it and I think my soul would be able to deal with it, although it might wince as it hovers above the room, seeing the dismemberment of a tiny but integral part of my body.

Chapter 27

Sex On The Golf Course

I only include this chapter for its tawdry, titillating factor. I have no personal interest in having sex on the golf course, where my mind is fully occupied on a different kind of stroke. But since well-meaning friends suggest its inclusion because of my passion for golf, I comment on it for its possibilities, improbable as it may be.

For one, where would you do it? The fairway is too open. The rough is too scratchy. Most courses don't have heavily wooded areas that provide privacy, just a few scraggly young trees that you can't even hide behind to relieve yourself

Some sand bunkers do have high lips and provide some coverage, but only from golfers on the other side of the fairway. You are fully exposed to players on the same side of the fairway as the bunker, and few are so deep that you are hidden below the surface of the fairway.

The tee box is definitely out. It is the most visible, even the championship tees, 'way in the back. I certainly wouldn't want to do it in a water hazard for health reasons; you don't know if there's leptorosis or other vile bacteria in them, let alone snakes or crocodiles.

The putting green is definitely out, since that is as visible as the tee box. Besides, with all the pesticides and insecticides used to keep the green green, you don't want them getting absorbed through the skin on your bottom or back.

The starter's office is definitely out, as is the pro shop, unless you can sneak into the rest room or dressing room. You could try it standing up with your clothes on but unzipped somewhere on the course, but you won't find much privacy anywhere on the golf course, including the tunnels from green to tee.

All in all, I'd say that the chances for privacy and opportunity are slim to none on the golf course. I suggest you wait until you get home, where you can institute your own 19th hole festivities.

Chapter 28

Sex For Dummies

By the time people get into their sixties and seventies and beyond, you'd think they'd wise up and have learned enough about life, themselves and others so they can have a fair amount of wisdom, experience and respect for others.

Unfortunately, some people don't get it, and perhaps never did, and do stupid things that are disrespectful, inconsiderate, and more importantly, are ineffective and unsuccessful and counter-productive to their aims, no matter how devious or lascivious.

Some reach what is called their mid-life crisis, and react erratically or ridiculously. The man in his fifties gets a flashy sports car or a toupee; the woman at whatever age gets a breast implant, face lift or liposuction. It can create tragic results – a man resorting to a comb-over with his few strands of hair kept long, combed over his otherwise balding head, or a woman with so much botox or so much makeup on that she cannot even smile, lest her face shatter.

For others, they resort to neurotic extremes to remain attractive. The older woman with a too-short skirt or with eyelashes so thick she can barely lift her eyelids to wink, rolling her eyes with a sidelong look, smiling seductively with a thick, flaming red lipstick that extends ½" beyond her thin lips. Or the man who wants to appear bold and confident, who approaches a desirable woman with what amounts to obscenities and clear overtones of his desire to have sex with her.

I think that most women, regardless of age, still want sex, just as men do, but they are looking for love and romance first. Sex comes later. They'll give sex to get love, whereas men will appear to give love to get sex. It will work some of the time for men, but if the women see through their intentions, it's all she-root.

Men should be courteous and attentive; no wandering eyes at the buxom woman at the next table. They should listen more than they talk, and ask more questions about her, her interests and her passions rather than go on about themselves. Which is not to mean they should offer no information about themselves. They can throw out a morsel about themselves, but should ask the woman to elaborate on what she just said, rather than expand on what they just said about themselves.

Some men talk about what they used to do for a living, what they now do to occupy their time, what hobbies they like, how much money they have (or insinuate they have), what they didn't like about their last wife, or how much they've traveled.

Which may be interesting, but you have to pay attention to your intention. If your intention is to get to know her better (for whatever nefarious purpose you may have), **you have to pay attention to her**.

- Get her to talk about herself.

- What does she like to do?

- What does she do to please herself?

- What are her plans for the rest of her life?

- What does she have on her bucket list?

- What does she like the most in a man?

You can steer clear of what her sign is, her favorite spiritual activity, what kind of books she likes to read (unless she says she LOVES to read), how many children she has, how many times she has been married, or how she feels about sex.

Take it slow and stick to what interests her. Let

her take the lead and nudge her to elaborate on her comments. If she says she loves to travel, ask her where her favorite spot is. On her next trip, does she want to go to some place new, or to some place she's already visited. What is her special interest for whatever answer she gave?

Get to know her as a person, and don't see her as the next woman you'd like to sleep with. Women are great at body language, and most women can see through insincerity and smell a fox on the prowl.

If you're tempted to throw out double entendres to a woman you've just met, don't. This will put her on guard, and she'll think you're either a clown or a boor. If she finds you attractive, she might find you funny and chalk you up as a prospect, but don't push it too early. Treat her with respect.

I once saw a guy who saw a striking woman, well-endowed, whose bosom was clearly featured in a tight-fitting sweater. I heard him approach her, a stranger, at the next table and asked with a Freudian slip, "May I borrow your sweater?"

Getting Her Into The Bedroom

No fast and hard rules about this one. The short version is, let things happen at their own pace, naturally. Don't rush her into it prematurely. You don't have to ask the most reserved, most genteel woman, especially a senior.

I would NOT suggest, "How about it, baby? I'm so hot for you I can't wait to get you into bed."

You don't have to ask, no matter how nicely or crudely, they'll let you know when they're ready, either by body language or directly.

A good friend of mine was dating the woman who was to be his second wife (he was a widower) shortly after her divorce. Although he was a gentleman with the ladies, he was as horny as they came.

After a few dates in which both found they were very compatible with each other, she asked him point blank, "When are we going to have sex?"

This is not a how-to manual, so I won't get into graphic details on how to seduce her or what techniques to use. After sex, though, despite your natural inclination (if you're the male) to roll over and go to sleep, your work is still not done. Your foreplay actually starts with post-sex, and you should engage in pillow talk, snuggle and cuddle, hold her in your arms and kiss her tenderly.

You don't have to French-kiss her and show how long your tongue is; tender, soft kisses will do. Not pecks on the cheek or lips, but let your lips linger on hers and with soft, slow, shallow flicks of your tongue. Kiss her tenderly and hold her close. Not tight enough to cut off her air supply, but close enough where she can feel your body warmth and to feel that you care. Tell her what it was like to make love with her (NOT what it was like having sex with her).

You don't have to throw in a perfunctory I-love-you unless you mean it, but you should let her know that you care about her and that you like her (at least).

Stroke her hair or her cheek and back. Caress her. If you "wham-bam, thanks, gotta go," you are not going to be welcomed for a reprise, unless you were SPECTACULAR.

Even then, you don't want to act as if it was strictly for the sex. Even if you're in it strictly for the sex, for God's sakes, treat her like a lady, with respect and sincerity. Be honest with her and don't mislead her by lies of omission or commission.

Basically, treat her with love and you'll get all the sex you can handle. Be prepared, though, you might discover you love her and want her for more than sex. And if you don't, man up and be honest with her. She might feel hurt at first, but she can decide if she wants to continue to have sex with you or if she wants to move on and is looking for a committed relationship.

If she feels the same way and is in it strictly for the sex, at least you're being heads-up with each other, and you'll end up as friends with fringe benefits, not a man and a woman playing games with each other. If it's the latter, you'll know you're conning each other, and sooner or later you'll know what the other knows, and it then becomes a neurotic game where the deceiver is the deceived, and vice versa, and you'll wonder if you're hanging around with someone that stupid or depraved, and you'll either feel that she's cheap, using you, or you sold yourself out.

So, keep it fair and honest. It's cleaner in the long run.

Chapter 29

STDs and AIDS

I knew a woman who was so assertive and health-aware that she asked men before she went to bed with them if they had taken tests for STD and AIDS and if they had their test results with them to show her they were negative. If they didn't, she said, sorry, see me when you can show that you're negative.

When I was single, I didn't have the chutzpah to do this, and took my chances. As you get to know a person better and are at a stage where you might start to get intimate, it's a good idea to bring the subject up. Nowadays, especially with AIDS, your ignorance could kill you. Even an STD could be an irritating inconvenience, and decommission you until it clears up.

Years ago while in a dentist's chair, I discovered to my alarm that my cold sore was herpes, simplex number one.

Now, whenever I feel a cold sore or blister on my

lower lip, I take acyclovir three times a day for a few days until it clears up.

I don't know how I got it or when, but it was sexually transmitted. I was told that it could lie dormant for years, then break out years later. Better to know than not know, better to play safe than be sorry.

After I found out (I was single then), following a full-disclosure policy, I told every woman I dated that I had herpes that might occasionally break out, and I would take some medication to treat it and would be fine in a few days. I never did ask my dates if they had taken tests for these diseases (didn't have the nerve), but since I didn't date at all for quite a while, it remained moot and academic.

It might be moot to pass on this caveat to your kids, who might be too old or too hip, but if they're single or divorced, it wouldn't be a bad idea to mention it to them. Or your grand kids, if they're old enough to be dating and are sexually active.

You might be too squeamish to bring this up with them, but it might open things up for you with them so they would feel free to talk to you about sex and to tap into your storehouse of wisdom based on your experience.

Or they might feel free to talk about other personal and intimate stuff, like their relationship with their boyfriend or girlfriend or spouse. Some serendipities might come your way.

Chapter 30

The Majority of One

Most, but not all of us, want to share the rest of our lives with someone rather than be alone. But even if you don't have a spouse or life partner, you can still lead a full and happy life, and be alone but not lonely.

Even if you have a spouse or life partner, you can feel lonely and that you're not leading a full and happy life. You have to be comfortable in your own skin, and know and love yourself.

No one has led a perfect childhood, and many if not all of us have had childhood trauma. Our actions are dictated by some childhood trauma and rely on some defense mechanism, something we did as a child that was then appropriate but may no longer be so, neither necessary nor in our best interests.

A woman who was raped by a large, black man in her youth may still be traumatized when alone with a large, black man in an elevator. A kid who fell from a tree or high place is afraid of heights as an adult, and may have an anxiety attack when in a glass elevator rising up in the exterior of a building. That fear response was appropriate earlier as a fight-or-flight reaction, but is no longer relevant nor appropriate, and the fear may linger on.

Therapy might help but isn't always necessary. Self-awareness may be all we need so we can adapt our behaviors more appropriate for us. As a child, our mother may have left us alone in an unlit room, and we may have felt frightened or abandoned when we awoke, slightly disoriented. Or she may have withheld her love because she wanted us to behave in a different way, and would only demonstrate her love when we acted in the way she wanted us to behave.

As adults, we may find ourselves trying to please others, forsaking what is good for us, so we won't feel abandoned or have those we love withhold their love or approval.

I forgot her name now, but a therapist pointed that you can be alone but don't have to be lonely. I used to belong to a singles club in Diamond Bar, California, named the Majority of One. They believed that you don't have to be in a relationship to be happy and fulfilled, that you can be by yourself (a majority of one) and lead a full and happy life.

You may prefer to be in a relationship to share experiences with someone dear to enrich your life, but it's not a prerequisite to be happy. Just knowing this and having others reinforce that belief took the pressure off ourselves to become one-half of a couple, and to stop seeing ourselves as incomplete.

Pursuing one's interests, doing what makes you happy, especially those activities not done in seclusion which expose you to others who are like-minded with the same interest, will put you in a position with people of similar interests. It doesn't have to be a big-time hobby or activity. Going to the library, supermarket, post office, shopping mall, restaurant, walking the dogs, going hiking or bicycling, going to the beach or mountains, traveling, having tea or coffee at a diner or coffee shop, going to the gym, taking dancing or yoga classes, are routine things you might do in your everyday life.

You might meet someone and engage in small talk, drop a friendly comment, and that might be the start of a friendship. It might be casual and not lead to anything, but they may introduce you to their friends, which might lead to something deeper.

Or none of these things may happen, but you are living your life the way you want, and that's what counts. You don't have to go out of your way to do different things with the express purposed of meeting THE ONE. Life is what happens while you're making plans for it, and you can enjoy the serendipities. Sometimes the things that happen are things we don't like or enjoy, like getting sick, but that might take you to the doctor's office or hospital, where you might meet someone interesting.

What happens to you is neither good nor bad. They just happen. We could be happy or sad, angry or disappointed, but these reactions are all a matter of choice. Sometimes they're unconscious, but they can be conscious decisions. If you choose to be happy rather than sad, you can become aware of your present feelings. You can then decide if you want to stay in your present state, stay in it for just a few minutes, or realize you are open to shifting to another mood now. And you'd rather be happy, you might conclude you may as well be happy now, choose accordingly, and get out of your funk.

As I said earlier, therapy can be helpful but not necessary to get to know yourself better. Looking at what negative moods come up for you, and under what conditions, you can ask yourself, What's the payoff if I get into that mood? There's always a payoff, even when it's not in your best interests.

For example, you might deduce that your mother or father may have made you feel worthless ("You're useless! You'll never amount to anything!"). You may feel that you lack self-worth, and must avoid others' disapproval in order to be loved. You may go against what you think is innately right for you because you want to please others and avoid their wrath, and that's your payoff for you.

Looking at it in this light, you might think, "That's silly. I'd rather be happier doing (whatever) instead. And I won't feel abandoned, or care if others approve or not. If they're my friends, they'll accept that as my preference. And if they don't, that's tough, and if they can't accept it, they're not really my friends."

Some people mistakenly think, I can be happy only if I'm in a relationship (or married). If I were married or in a relationship, then I'd be happy or I can do (draw up your list).

The other side of the coin is, I can be happy if I were doing the things I like, such as (draw up your list). Note that this list is not dependent on your being married or in a relationship.

Maybe your life would be richer if shared, but it's not an imperative. And that's the reality, and the nice thing about it.

Chapter 31

A Happily Married Sex Addict

Technically, a sex addict is addicted to sex, and wants to nail everything that isn't nailed down, even if the other party is married, engaged or in a relationship, as long as it has a pulse. They not only love sex but are hooked on it, like a smoker is to nicotine, and can't help themselves.

The trick with a married person is to be hooked only to his or her spouse, in which they can be categorized as a sex maniac or permanently horny spouse. Which is a nice thing to be, and is likely to be infectious; the spouse may become a sex addict, hooked only to their spouse.

Things could get so out of control that they seek partners outside of their marriage. It could get nasty and lead to divorce. It sounds awfully inept to say that you couldn't help yourself when you get caught sleeping with a good friend of your spouse's.

I don't know what the conventional cure is,

and most may recommend counseling or therapy, but I would strongly recommend against aversion therapy. The treated person may develop an aversion to sleeping with his or her spouse, and may even develop an aversion to masturbation, an outlet for the person's pent-up emotions.

I don't know what the answer is to this potentially serious problem. In creating great sex, you don't want to create a Frankenstein with an insatiable appetite which you cannot satisfy. I guess too much of a good thing can be dangerous, but think of what it will do to enhance your reputation. That is, if you can handle it.

Chapter 32

Does Sex Make You Hard of Hearing?

At my good friend Ron's wedding on January 29, 2011, despite the fact that this was his third wedding (he was widowed twice), when the pastor got to the part, "Do you, Ron, take Jane as your lawfully wedded wife?" Perhaps out of nervousness or because he's hard of hearing, he asked, "Come again?"

Prior to that, perhaps to speed things up, when the pastor said, "I can offer you two versions. The long version is where I get more into the biblical references, and –"Ron interrupted, "I'll take the short version."

Chris and I have a running gag. Because I speak in a barely audible voice, she often doesn't hear me and I have to repeat myself. And I am often inattentive and don't catch her first words, and have to admit, "What did you say? I didn't hear you."

Instead of getting irritated at each other, the in-house joke is, "Don't you know that too much or too little sex can make you hard of hearing?"

And the usual retort is, "What did you say?"

Tonight, Amanda was over for dinner and asked if we were going to take the dogs for a W-A-L-K. The dogs have a vocabulary and know what "walk" means, and get hyper at its mention, so we usually spell it out, like parents do before their young children.

Chris replied, "No, it's already dark, but I'm going to give them a T-R-E-A-T." I was sitting at an adjoining chair and not on the sofa with them, and laughed out loud and asked, "What did you just spell out?"

They both laughed because it seemed as if I didn't know what the letters spelled out, even after Chris repeated herself.

I laughed and said, "What did you just spell out? I didn't get it."

They laughed and Chris spelled it out again. This time I roared with laughter and said, "I didn't hear the R."

At which they laughed again, and Amanda said it was time for her to go, and would leave us alone.

Chapter 33

Drive Your Woman Wild In Bed

Every guy has the idea it would be nice to have a great sex life.

The **knee-jerk responses** would be stuff like:

- Give her oral sex until she has an orgasm.

- Play out her most erotic fantasy for her.

- Make love to her under the stars.

- Cover the bed with freshly cut flowers.

- Have a fire going and put iced champagne in a bucket.

- Let her cover you with strawberries and whipped cream, and eat you for dessert.

- Watch an erotic video in bed together.

- Caress her with your mouth and fingers in her erogenous zones.

- Kiss her on the neck, lower back, below her navel and inner thighs before you kiss her on the mouth.

- Fondle her breasts, tweaking her nipples between your thumb and index finger.

The more pragmatic and probable answers would be:

- Eat crackers in bed.

- Do a crossword puzzle while she lies there in her sexy lingerie.

- Watch a late night talk show on TV in bed.

- Read any book, especially an erotic one, while she lies there naked next to you.

- Cut your toenails in bed.

- Do your tax returns early.

- Get a mirror and tweezers and pluck your nostril hairs.

- Watch a History or Discovery Channel TV show.

- Check your e-mails on your laptop.

- Write a long letter to your ex-wife or ex-girlfriend.

-

Chapter 34

How To Stay Attractive To Women

Women are most attracted by men with resources and status, and the men most likely to have them are successful senior men, although there are boy billionaires nowadays due to electronic phenomena (google, amazon, etc.) who truly have it all.

Most, however, are no longer ab-ripped, wide-shouldered, slim-waisted hunks with smoldering eyes and curly locks, but they have experience, patience, wisdom and perspective, and if they are reasonably fit and especially if they have money, women will find them attractive.

A man over 60 or 70 has an enormous pool of women to choose from, since women outlive men and the ratio of women to men favor the men. Most older women aren't looking for a boy toy.

They want someone they can talk to , who has status, who's somebody and who has accomplished something, for with all the trappings they usually have more money at their command.

To be classy, you can brag modestly. If they talk about travel, if you've been to the same places, say so, and ask if they ate at a famous restaurant there or if they stayed at a ritzy hotel you're familiar with, just to subtly let them know of your station in life.

If you have one, don't be afraid to wear your Rolex instead of your Casio or Timex.

Women seek an affable companion, not a meal ticket. Listen attentively to what they say.

Don't just let them talk, listen to what they have to share with you. Ask follow-up questions. Look like you mean it. You don't have to look like a 20-year-old kid. Just show that you haven't given up and want to look fit.

At your age, your wrinkles give you character. You've earned them and wear them as a badge of honor. You don't have to dye your hair jet-black or graft patches of hair over your bald spot. Be proud of the gray or silver in your hair. If you don't like your bald spot, shave your head. It often adds character and gives you a more masculine look. (At least, tell yourself that.)

The best way to appear attractive to women is to find them attractive, and show it in as many ways as you can. They don't want a kid, they want a man. And if they want a boy toy or be a cougar, take a pass and move on. There are plenty of fish in the ocean (more senior females than males), and if you show that you're not clingy or needy, and are confident enough to look elsewhere, they might find you more attractive and may not be willing to let go of a good thing.

It doesn't hurt to care about your appearance and dress neatly. You don't have to dress like a male fashion model, but a neat, nattily dressed man is more attractive than a man of the same age and build who dresses like a slob or is careless about his appearance. Be neatly shaved or have your facial hair trimmed neatly.

An upright posture rather than a slouched one is eye-appealing, and someone with a sprightly walk and confident stride is more eye-catching than one who shuffles his feet and looks like he needs a walker or a cane.

It doesn't take much money to look your best and to dress for success, even as a retiree. Take stock of yourself and spruce up.

Chapter 35

When She Says, "We Need To Talk."

According to one study, when a woman says, "We need to talk," she has a complaint, usually about her relationship with her partner or his sexual performance. From my limited experience, it usually signifies that the woman has been mulling over something, pored over the pros and cons, had already made up her mind about the issue, and is ready to announce her decision, unilaterally.

It could mean that she feels she has not been heard, or heard but not heeded, is ready to break up, or wants clarification over something because her interpretation has her tied up in knots.

All I know is, when I hear these words, my antennae go up and I'm expecting the worst.

I've never heard good news following it. However, I note that I've been blind-sided by all kinds of stunning bad news without so much as a prefatory "we have to talk."

So, whenever you hear a women open her mouth, you can expect anything and everything. All you can be sure of, she has parted her lips. When a woman says, "We need to talk," I do NOT expect to hear:

1. I'm in love with you.

2. I'm pregnant! Do you want a boy or a girl?

3. I need to take a pee. Where's the bathroom?

4. Do you have any laxatives in the house?

5. You don't say "excuse me" when you fart.

Chapter 36

What Does It Mean Now That We Had Sex?

I've never been in this situation, so all I can do is conjecture as to what might transpire. I think it's a natural question that a man will ask himself.

For me, it would sound as if he will:

- Give up his freedom and have to start planning things to include her.

- Assess what kind of relationship he wants with her.

- Bring up the subject with her to see what her take is of the situation.

- Assess for himself what kind of relationship he wants.

- Thanks-but-adios, one-time-only, strictly for sex, light, casual, exclusive, or serious.

My assessment is more like this:
Since you did have sex, **one or more of the following were in effect**:

- Great attraction, chance opportunity.

- Pure lust.

- Mutual lust.

- One or both were horny and lonely or bored.

- Love at first sight.

- Destiny.

- Cupid was at work.

At any rate, it either grows or dies, or stays the same. The latter is awkward; you're in limbo, and won't do either of you any good.

Chapter 37

How Not To Hit Below The Belt
(Even If You Want To)

The time sequence is jumbled, but nearly two years after our marriage, we saw a counselor. Even though we get along well 95% of the time, when we have fights or flare-ups, the intensity and shock of the pain and anger seem to outweigh in impact all the times when we are in harmony and deeply in love.

What we learned (or were told) is that we are not our anger, thoughts and feelings; they are not our authentic selves, who love each other and don't want to hurt each other, and that we only want to continue to love each other.

When we fight or have flare-ups, we lose our consciousness and all our conditioned reflexes come up automatically, and we react in the same old way we have in the past, which have not served us well before or now.

The counselor usually says that fights are NOT

normal and are avoidable; that we should welcome the opportunity to face our next fight/flare-up; and that we should just do one simple thing (actually, three): Take notice of what is happening in our body, what we are thinking, and what we are feeling. Just remain conscious, avoid going unconscious (not thinking), and avoid going into our conditioned reflexes.

We may not like what the other is saying or what we're hearing, but only note what's happening in our bodies, our minds, and our feelings. Take note if you're reacting to what was said or how it was said, but focus on what is in the heart of the other person – not by asking the person to be more specific about the message, but what is in the heart of the person.

The key note is to PRACTICE this; it may take a while to get the hang of it. When you find yourself reacting emotionally, physically or mentally to whatever you think was communicated, focus on what is in the HEART of the person. Put yourself in that person's shoes, and empathize what that person is going through.

Use "empathy" statements, not "I feel" statements. Say "I hear what you're saying..." Don't correct factual errors or misperceptions; that's for another time.

Believe that fights and flare-ups can be a thing

of the past and need not be put up with or repeated. They can be eliminated. PRACTICE.

Chapter 38

Keep Your Hand out of the Cookie Jar

My wife has lots of interesting and attractive friends, many of them married. Because they love her, they greet me with open arms and are very cordial, expecting and giving hugs and kisses.

I'm used to that. We did the same thing in Hawaii. As in Hawaii, most are younger than I, some much younger, by 10 to 20 years. Even my past wives were much younger, 10, 9 and 18 years younger.

Some of them greet me enthusiastically and warmly. While it's not sexual, it does stir my libido, though they don't know it. It takes a little effort to acknowledge my physical reaction, and I have to remind myself that I'm married and these are her friends – well, actually, ours – and they're not coming on to me.

Sometimes, in hugging them back, without thinking, my hands slip dangerously close to where they shouldn't go, and I have to raise them to a more appropriate height so it won't be misconstrued as intentional groping.

Of course, the more attractive and enthusiastic the hugger, the more at-risk I am at misbehaving.

Not that I'd do anything if any of them did come on to me, invitingly. Being impotent, it would be foolhardy of me to initiate anything since I couldn't deliver on what may look like an invitation.

So, it's easy for me to be loyal, faithful and trustworthy, and I can clinically observe their attractiveness and friendliness, and continue to be a good chum and enjoy their company.

Having a great wife doesn't hurt. And I do take my marriage vows seriously, and wouldn't risk what we have for a dalliance.

Besides, if she caught me, she'd cut my hands off, or other parts of my body, and I'd never hear (or see) the end of it. I'd have a better chance as an alcoholic, which I used to be before I quit in 1979.

She also has eyes in the back of her head. A month or so ago, I shook the hand of an attractive woman in our astrology class. When I met her, I shook her hand held her by the right forearm with my left hand, and when I left, we hugged and I again held her by the right forearm with my left hand. My wife commented on it later, that I had touched her twice.

Thank goodness I'm remaining faithful by choice. If I ever THOUGHT of it, she'd probably tell me, "I know what you're thinking. Don't try it – or else."

Chapter 39

Fantasy Fantasies

In my ideal fantasy world, I'm forever young, 6' tall with a 32" waist, six-pack abs, boyishly handsome with eyes hinting at wisdom beyond my years. I speak clearly and confidently, in a bold voice that can be forceful when needed, soft and sensitive when appropriate, well to do though not necessarily wealthy, and drive a nice but not offensively opulent car.

I have a home of similar appearances – bigger than it looks, smaller than its expensive features suggest, with a modest exterior but striking interiors and a fabulous view. I'm happily married and congenial with a small, not wide, circle of friends, and we socialize in each other's homes.

We come from different walks of life but are comfortable with each other because of our shared values and interests. We all appreciate beauty and the arts, and golf as well; although I don't excel at all of them.

Having said that, it hardly describes my real-life situation. I'm old, have a paunch and bald spot, speak in a barely audible voice, and we use my wife's car (I don't have one). I moved into her home, which is lovely. I love her dearly, and we do have a small circle of interesting and fascinating friends. We are somewhat esthetic but not raving fanatics about the arts, and I suck at golf, which I love.

And though I try to lose weight and get more trim, and try to get better at golf, my life is just fine even if nothing changed. I would still be frustrated when I step on the scales or am on the golf course, flailing away, but life is good. It's good to be grounded in reality and make the most of what I've got, and to appreciate what I have and to be grateful for that. And now, if you'll excuse me, I have to answer my e-mail from Publisher's Clearing House so I can win the $10 million sweepstakes.

Actually, I'd settle for $5,000 a week for life, even if it means living on a budget.

Chapter 40

Is Sex Overrated?

From the pulpits at church to every psychologist and psychiatrist, and to marriage counselors everywhere, and to every commercial you see on the tube, you'd think that the world thinks about sex every 30 seconds, and are doing it as frequently as possible. I may be in the minority (which I am, racially speaking), but I don't think it's the driving force among many of the married people in my age bracket.

To protect the silent celibate among us, I won't mention any names, and I haven't asked them point blank if they do or don't or how often they do it.

Women do talk among themselves, or have their built-in antennae and sensory devices peculiar to their gender, and my wife says with unquestionable authority that this couple hasn't slept together in years, and that couple sleeps in separate bedrooms, and by other means and senses that women seem to possess unbeknownst to the simple-minded men, she KNOWS.

No one knows for sure what's really going on between a husband and wife, but the couples we know all seem to have adjusted to each other after many years of marriage, not all of them smooth, some actually bumpy, and they interact with each other with congeniality and familiarity.

Not always in a lovey-dovey way; in fact, sometimes, there's a clear line of irritability and accepted testiness, with expressions like, "So you can read my mind and know what I'm thinking, so you can finish my sentence?

I was going to talk about the Indian artifact, not that painting." Or, "I had to switch him away from tennis to golf before he gets another heart attack, and I don't need that."

Despite the apparent dissatisfaction with the spouse's decisions and their need for intercession, behind it all is an obvious concern for their well-being and sincere love, where they don't want their spouses to put themselves at risk.

Some of these couples, many of whom have been together for decades and decades, though they obviously love each other, do not even hold hands in public or give each other a peck or a smooch in front of others. But by their speech and general disposition, it's clear they have settled in for the long haul, and are very comfortable with each other.

With some couples, it's clear to see that if one has a serious health problem that is life-threatening, the other would not want to go on alone without the spouse, and would die shortly thereafter, or would be totally bereft and unable to cope on their own.

They may or may not be sexually active, but their love for each other is written all over their faces and how they interact with each other, often with no physical contact between them.

If the husband has health issues, such as hypertension, impotency, erectile dysfunction, or an enlarged prostate which prevents them from having sex, the wives have accepted their lot and adjusted for that, and adapted to a way of marital life that doesn't threaten their feelings of intimacy and their love for each other.

So, I believe that sex is overrated for the older generation, and they're not missing a thing. They are leading rich, fulfilled lives, and happy with their lot.

Let the younger ones hoot and cavort and rattle the headboards, and go at it multiple times a week. Like a sports car driver who has eased into a comfortable and sedate sedan in his later years, the older generation has been there, done that, and content with their lot in life.

They can act their own age and to their own expectations, and not conform to Madison Avenue's or television's depiction on what kind of sex life they should have.

And that is how it should be –according to their own standards and needs, not anyone else's. More power to us older folks!

To Contact the author or purchase books:

George Kagawa
e-mail: georgekagawa@gmail.com

Glorybound Publishing
439 S. 6th St. Camp Verde AZ 86322
928-567-3340
www.gloryboundpublishing.com
or Amazon.com

Made in the USA
Las Vegas, NV
12 December 2023

82704947R10090